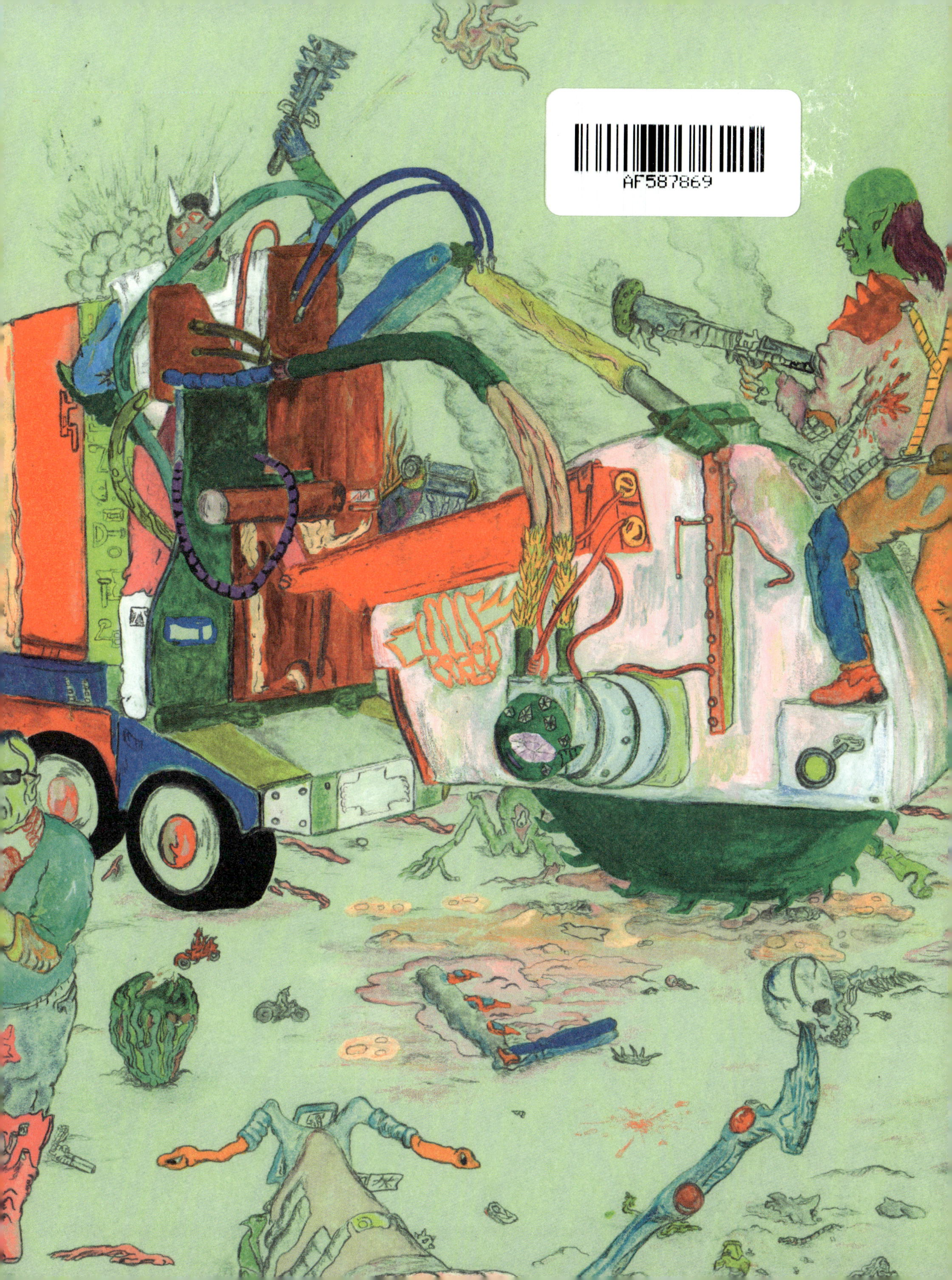

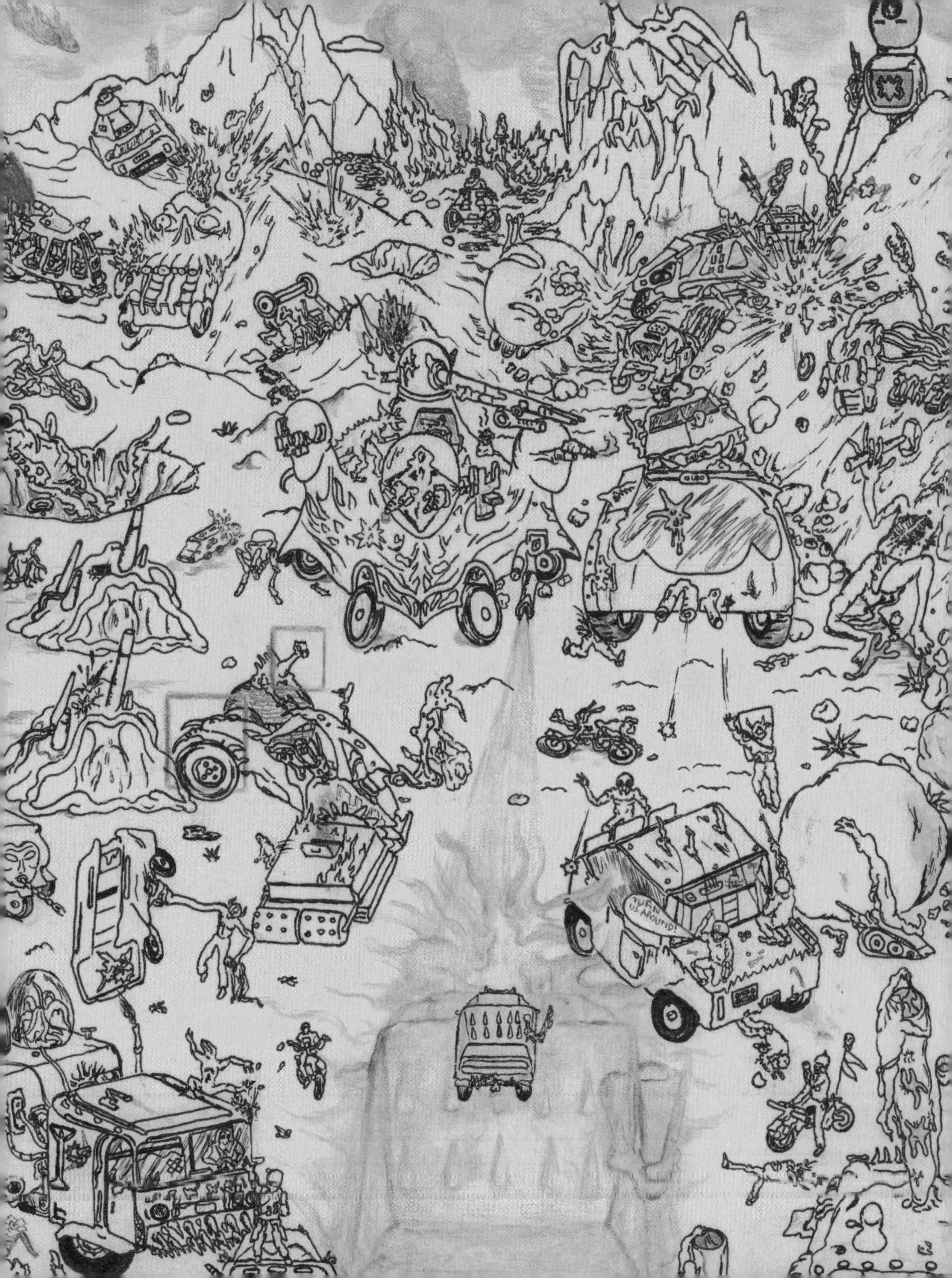
TURN US AROUND!

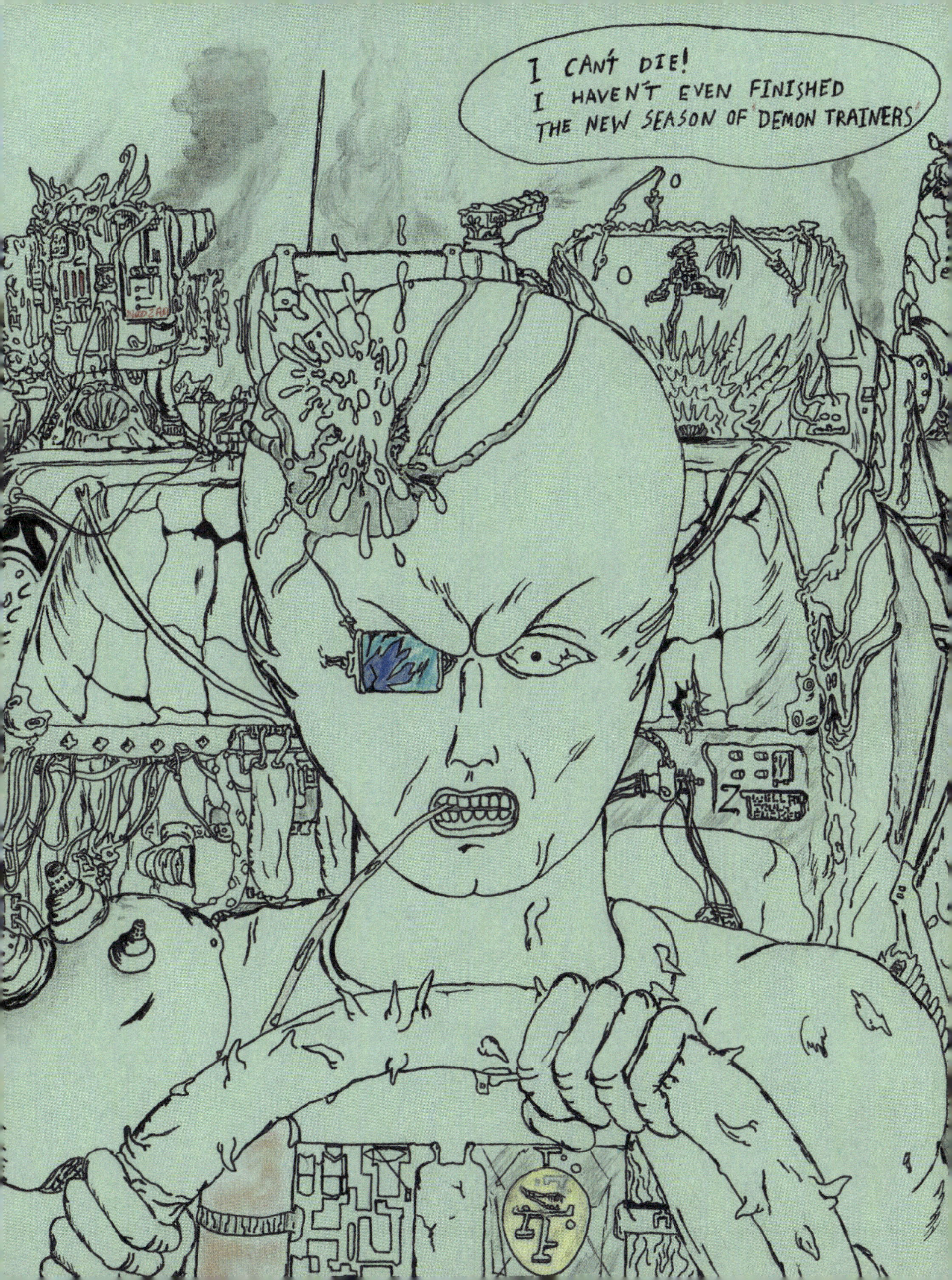
I CAN'T DIE!
I HAVEN'T EVEN FINISHED
THE NEW SEASON OF 'DEMON TRAINERS'

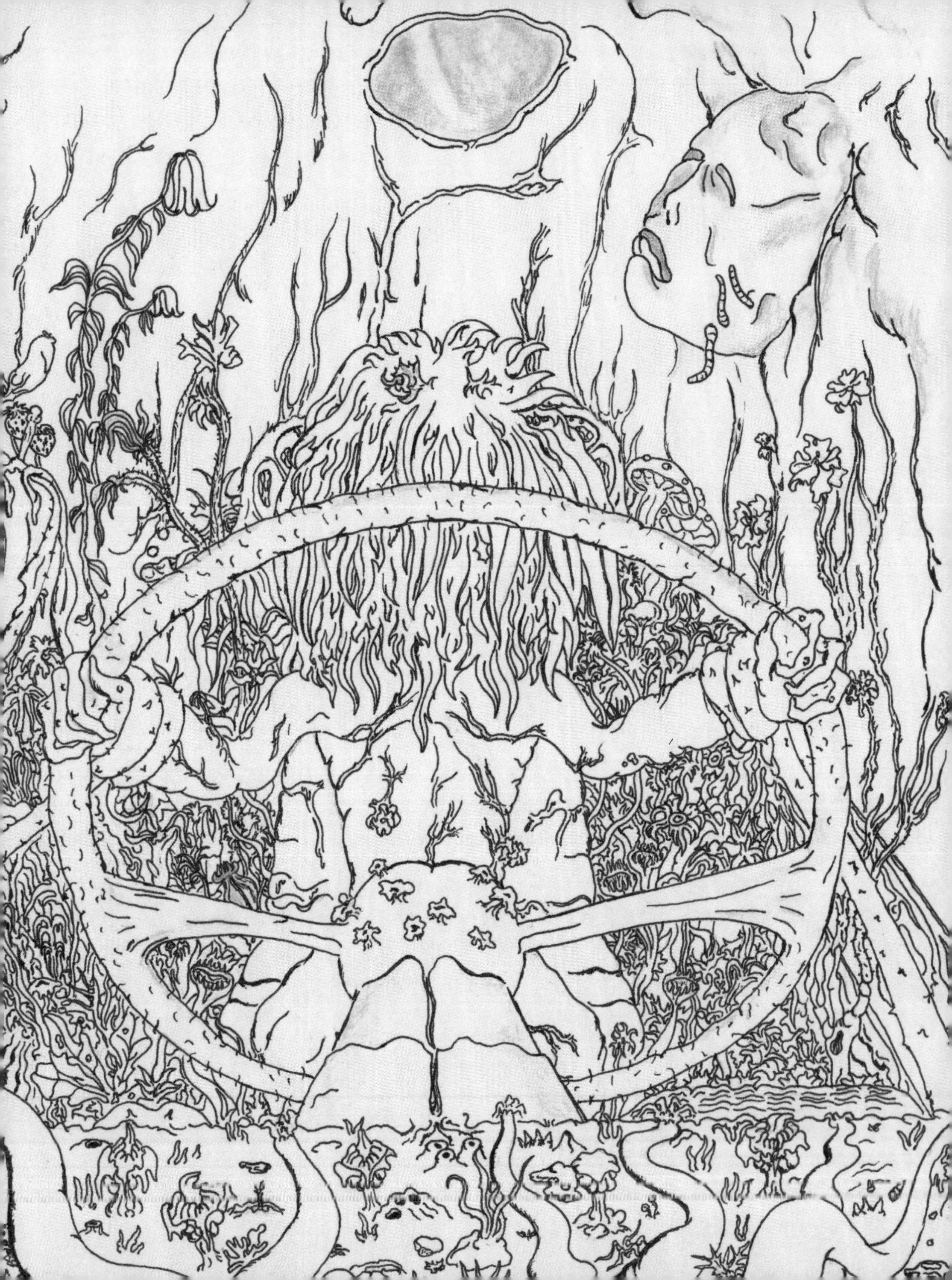

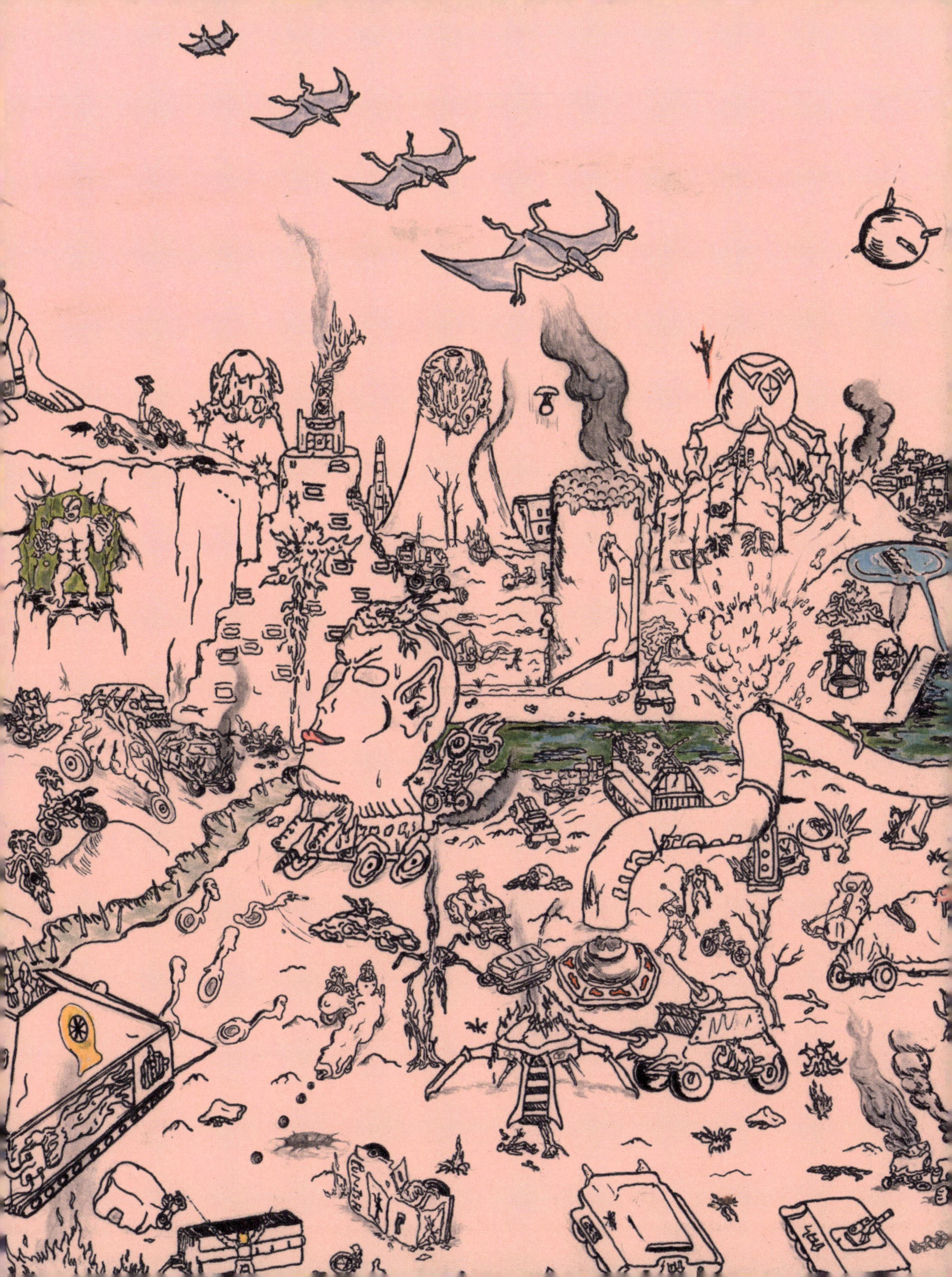

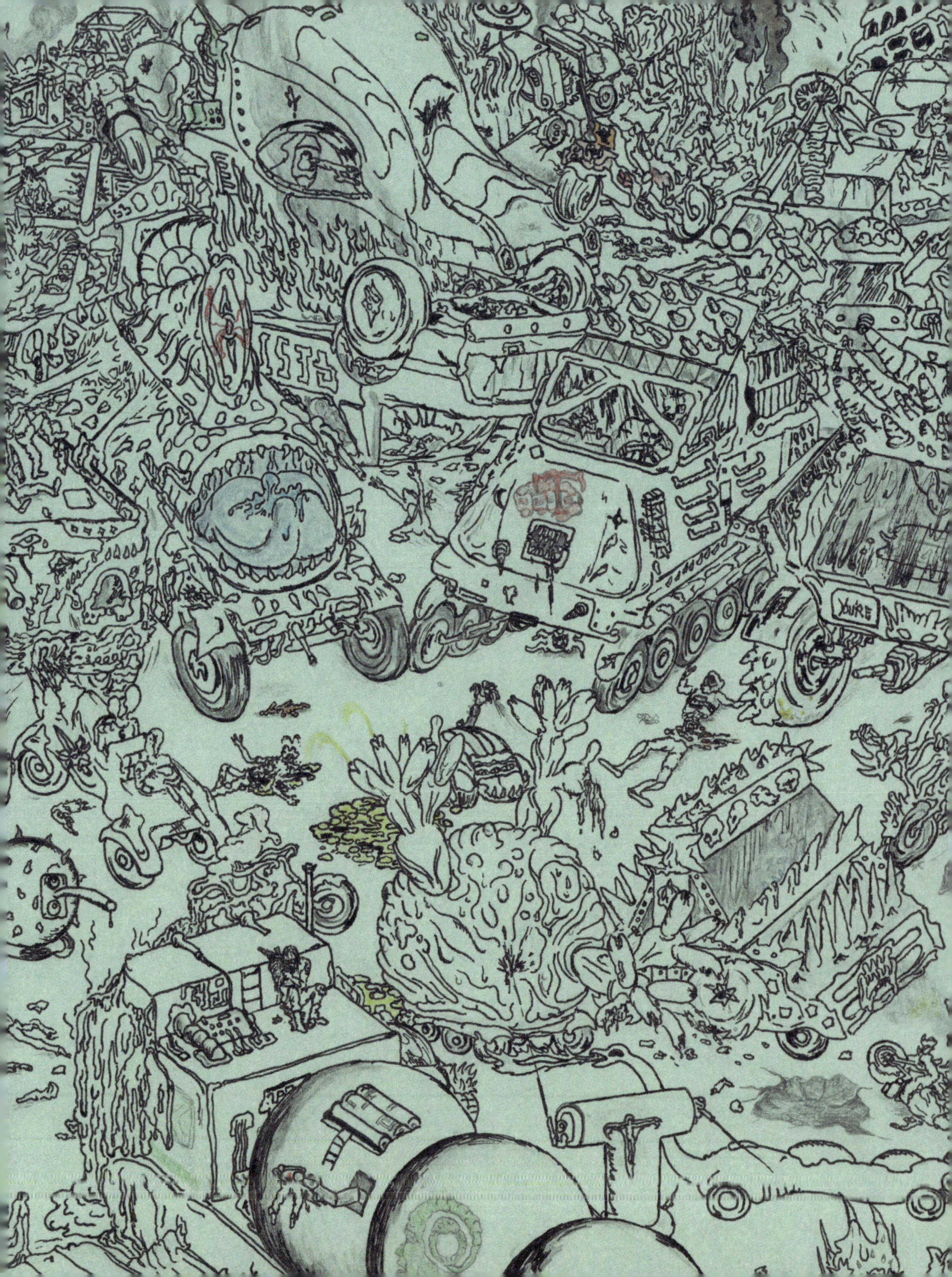
YOU'RE

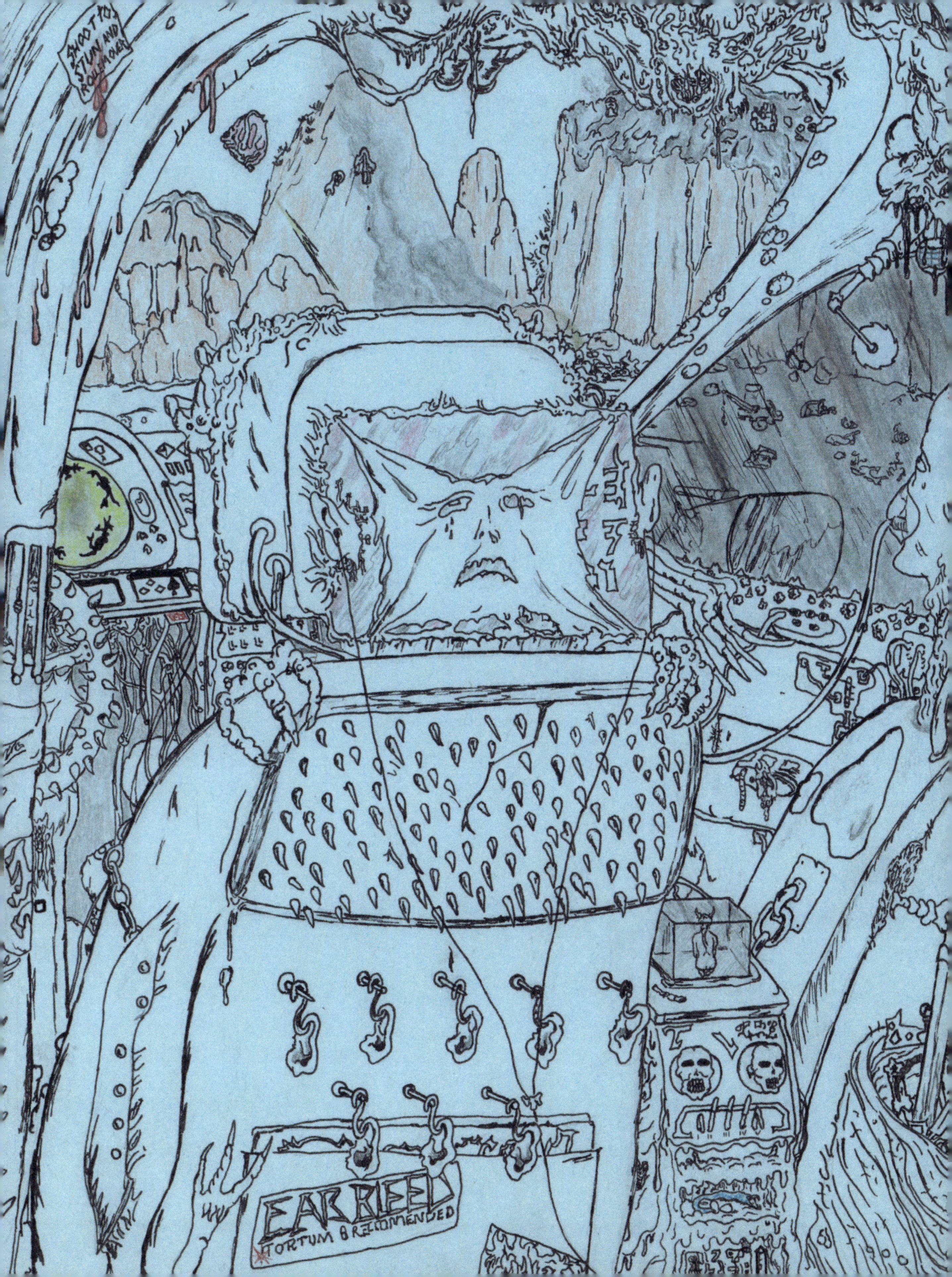
SHOOT TO STUN AND ROLL OVER
EAR REEL
TORTUM B RECOMMENDED

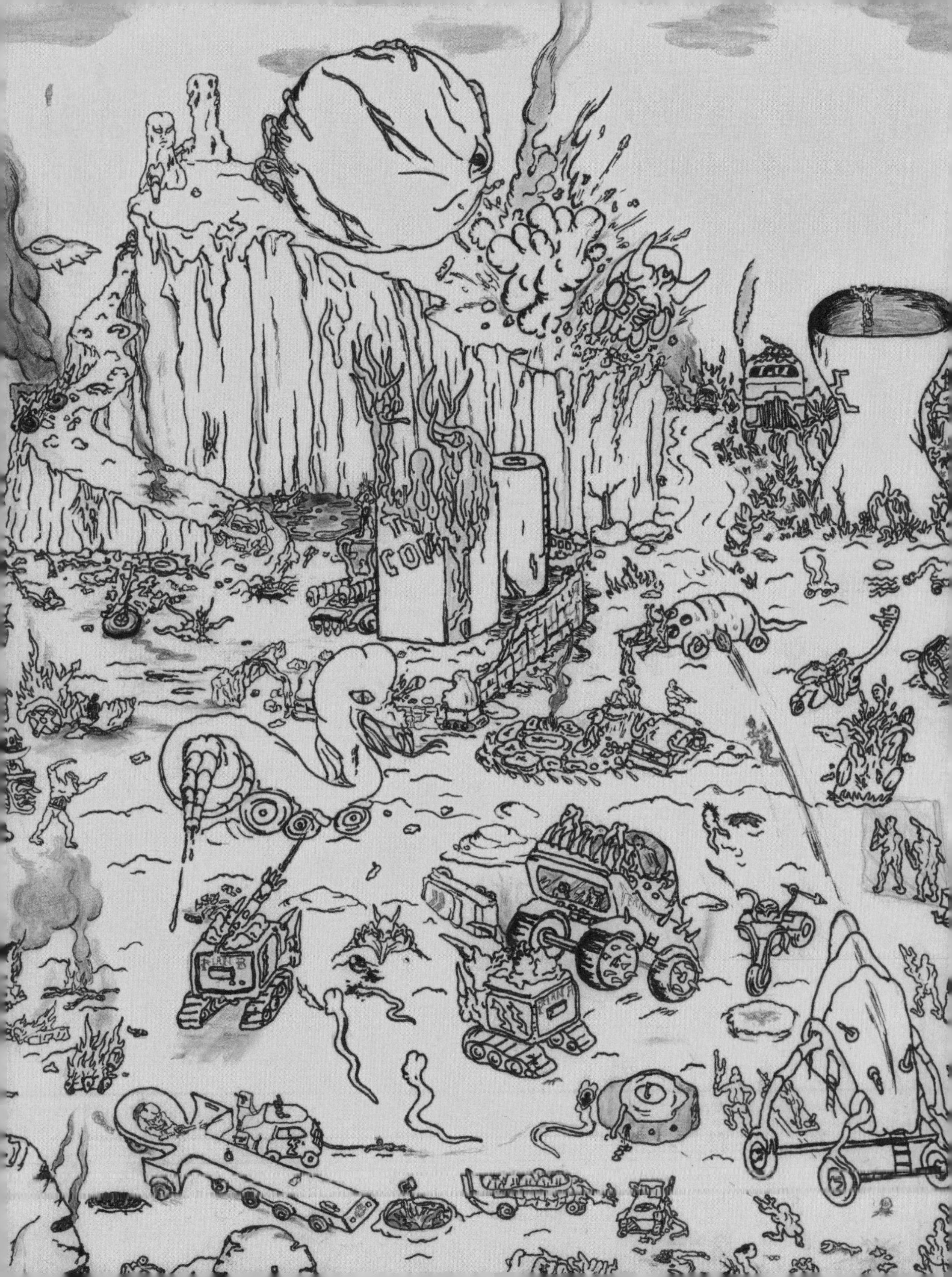

PLAN B
PLAN A
TERROR

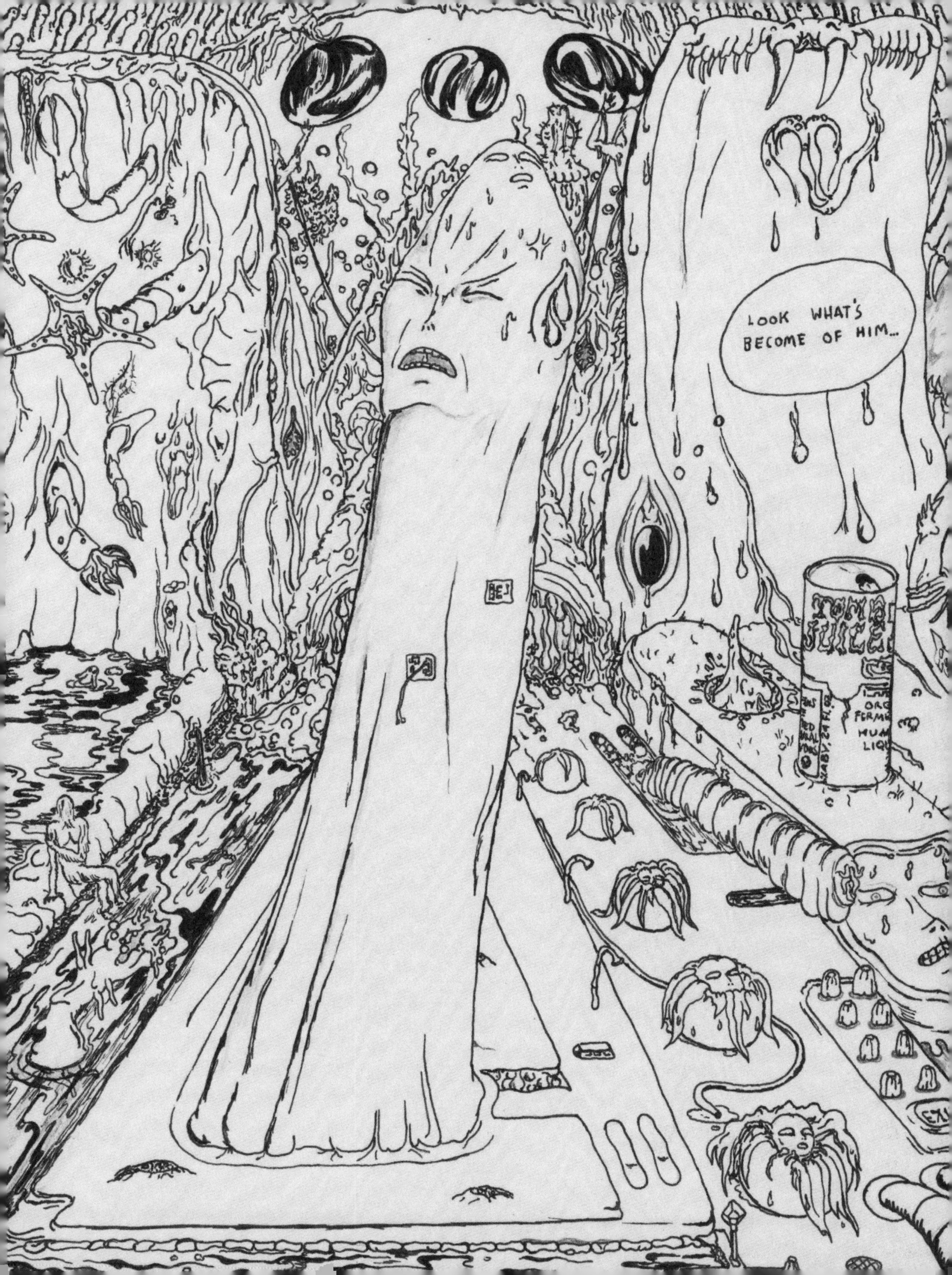

LOOK WHAT'S BECOME OF HIM...

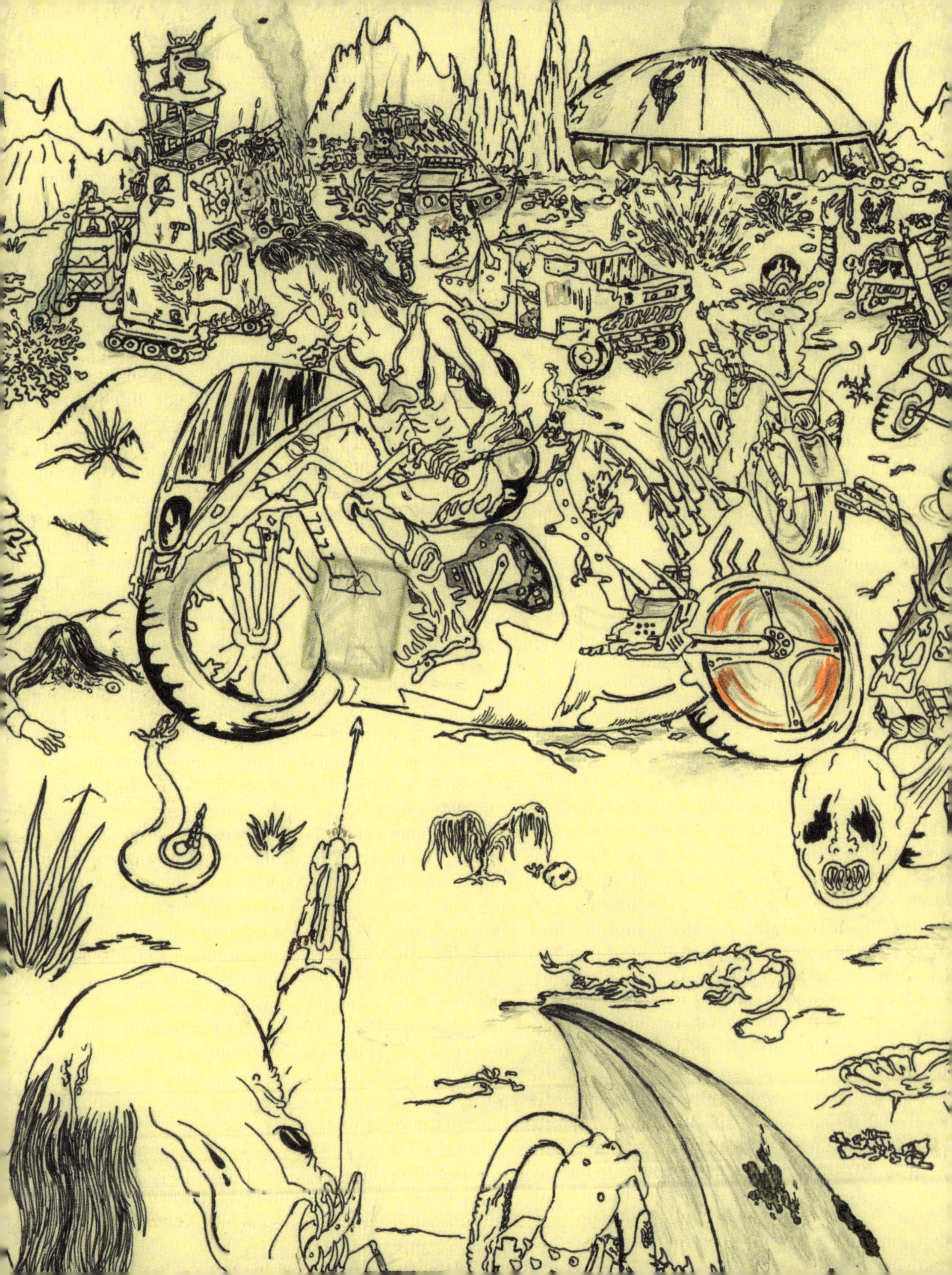

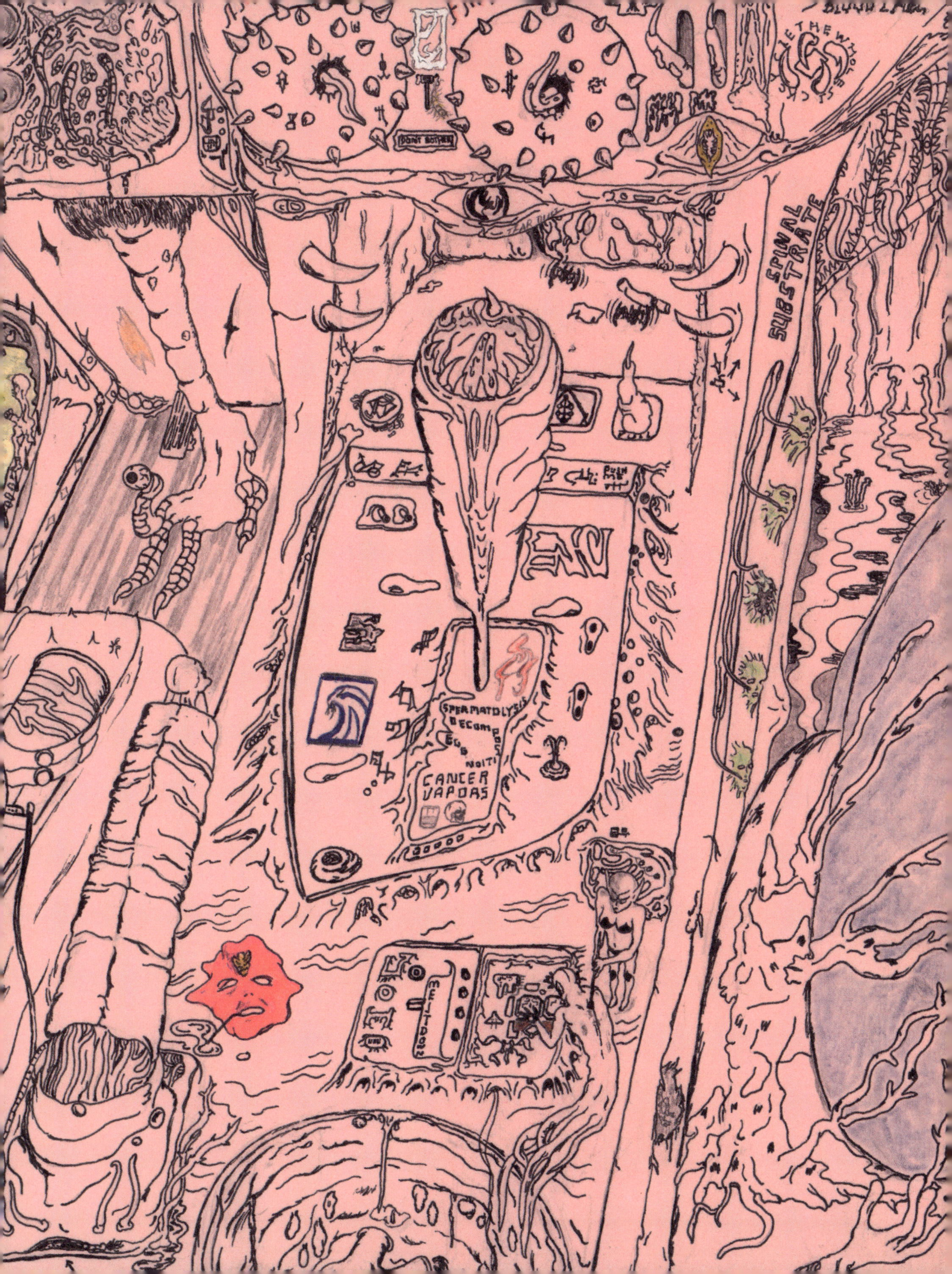
SPINAL SUBSTRATE
SPERMATOLYSIS
CANCER
VAPORS

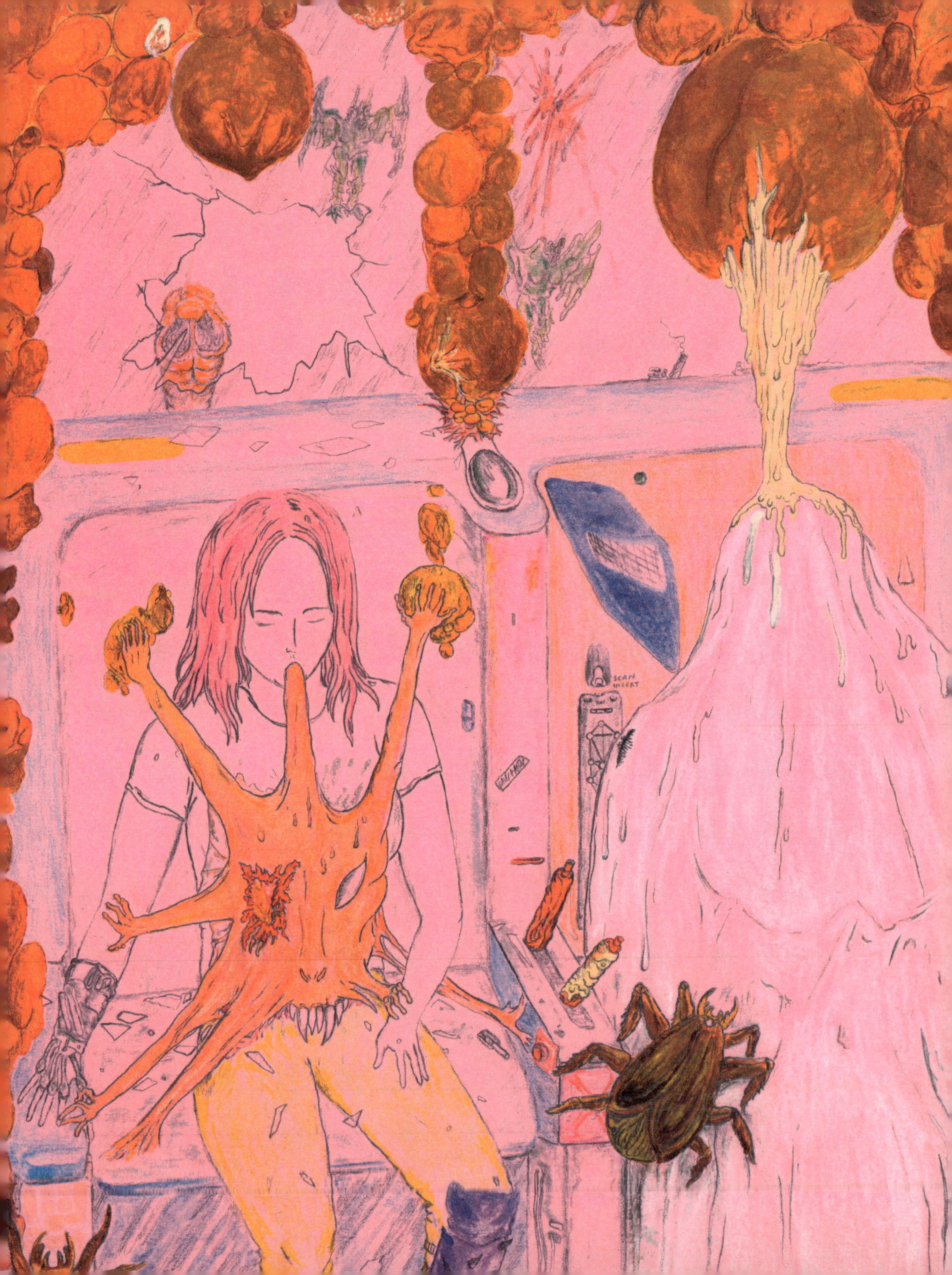
SCAN
INSERT